AF413782

BY FATIMAH ASGHAR

If They Come for Us
When We Were Sisters
Daughter of the Mountains

DAUGHTER
OF THE
MOUNTAINS

DAUGHTER OF THE MOUNTAINS

POEMS OF HEARTBREAK
& HOMECOMING

Fatimah Asghar

ONE WORLD
NEW YORK

One World
An imprint of Random House
A division of Penguin Random House LLC
1745 Broadway, New York, NY 10019
oneworldlit.com
penguinrandomhouse.com

A One World Trade Paperback Original

Copyright © 2026 by Young Aunties Inc.

Penguin Random House values and supports copyright. Copyright fuels creativity, encourages diverse voices, promotes free speech, and creates a vibrant culture. Thank you for buying an authorized edition of this book and for complying with copyright laws by not reproducing, scanning, or distributing any part of it in any form without permission. You are supporting writers and allowing Penguin Random House to continue to publish books for every reader. Please note that no part of this book may be used or reproduced in any manner for the purpose of training artificial intelligence technologies or systems.

ONE WORLD and colophon are registered trademarks of Penguin Random House LLC.

ISBN 978-0-593-97993-8
Ebook ISBN 978-0-593-97994-5

Printed in Canada

9 8 7 6 5 4 3 2 1

BOOK TEAM: Production editor: Cara DuBois • Managing editor: Rebecca Berlant, Allison Fox • Production manager: Sandra Sjursen • Proofreaders: Erika Bruner, Olivia Trzaski

INTERIOR ART: Yulia Druzenko/Adobe Stock

The authorized representative in the EU for product safety and compliance is Penguin Random House Ireland, Morrison Chambers, 32 Nassau Street, Dublin D02 YH68, Ireland. https://eu-contact.penguin.ie

for Allah,
my greatest friend

& for my ancestors,
guides & spirit team

& the beings who know me more
than i know myself

DAUGHTER
OF THE
MOUNTAINS

in 2025 Pakistan proposed a ban prohibiting "supernatural practices,"
claiming them to be "black magic" & "anti-Islamic" & dangerous.
this is part of an increased state surveillance of any form of spirituality
that's not mainstream Wahhabism.

in Pakistan, indigenous people, practices & religious minorities —
including Buddhists, Hindus, Christians, Sufis, Shias, Ahmadis,
Ismailis & syncretic folk-Islamic practitioners—are policed as an
attempt to relegate Pakistan's history to the start of the modern
nation-state (in 1947) & to distance the nation from any history
that predates Islam.

the criminalization of spirituality outside mainstream orthodoxy
erases indigeneity, warps cultural memory & divorces us from
land & belonging.

oh, Allah
great story
great creator
great mystery

verily,
i release
all stories
i carry
that keep
me from
seeing

verily,
i release
what i thought
i knew

what i clung to
what i built my boat
out of
to survive
the crashing sea

verily,
i welcome
in the divine

verily,
i welcome
in what's real

verily,
i welcome
in what's here

& what's ready
to be heard

i. daughter of [the return]

at the edge of an edge
is an edge. at that edge
is a cliff. beyond that cliff
is me.

[in the time before borders]

you could walk from europe to hind

in the time where faith melted into faith

& the indus swelled to push back sikander.

alexander the great, but not here. he came

& we prayed & the rivers answered.

beaten back by water, an army lost to the swell

that said no. goat's milk gifted to the raavi

to stop the zamindars from collecting

fruits of others.

+

now, the raavi littered with candy wrappers.

now, the indus shrunk miles from her

bed. now, the two-hundred-year-old boat lives

on land, a field under the rust. now, the forest

cut to make homes, now, the borders carved

through mountain only the horsemen can cross.

how holy, the river—

+

how holy, the forest, what knowing kept in the leaves

of the trees. between the rocks, the mantras

were given for the buddhists, for the hindus,

for the muslims, the same spirits sewing the thread

of their hearing, eyeing those who'd honor their call. a thousand

poems, a thousand prayers, saplings, falling like couplets.

+

do you know its many names? blinded, would you raise

your sword to the tree who knew your grandmother's

skin? where your god sang & different ears named

it their own? call it yaksha/ nature spirit/ tree-fairy/

jinn/ (mis) translated through the words of humans.

spirit/ spirit/ spirit/ by a different name.

[armor]

musk from karbala, oud
lingering. what smell keeps
the jinn away, what smell
invites them in. summer jasmine
& winter amber, sweet & thick
riding in the language of wind.
rose petals & salt tucked in news
-papers, sand from the slaughter
hardened to tasbeehs, glass bangles
yaqoot & firoza, ocean stone
pressed into ring. my family stacked
me with stories,
taweez, chilies over my head
rotating seven times & burned
in the fire. smell or no smell,
who gave me the look, what face
comes in the flame. little amulet
carried in my wallet, bits
of earth prayed over & torn.
i arm myself with what
the land gave, i arm myself
with my tongue, quick to spit
a surah or a curse. not thinking,
i slash into a pomegranate & there's
a massacre on the table. blood

& no seeds to eat. after watching
the youtube video, i cut with
the precision of an aunty. the fruit
gifts for days. plump seeds
the color of yaqoot. with respect,
everything permissions. touched
the right way, even poison ivy won't sting.
call it by its true name & the world
opens. yes, reader. even to you.

[someone was born]

then fled & birthed another.

someone moved & moved & moved.

fled again.

someone loved the land & someone didn't.

someone knew & then someone forgot.

the knowing left like a small butterfly, gentle.

before anyone could realize it was gone.

someone kept moving.

someone finally looked back & asked, where?

[when i ask the mountains]

where i'm from they show
me strings, soft & silken, yes,

but still there, edging my fingers.
fake puppeteer, trying to sway
a charmed god

a god to whom i promised surrender
& then buckle my blood when
the world doesn't go my way. i come

from a long line of ants, delusional,
confusing dirt for clouds.
my ancestors made lists

of what to do & what not to.
safety is an illusion, my partner says
after the police raid our cabin

hands raking through our things.
when we tell our friends we're met
with a litany: *you should've.*

you should've. you should've:
not gone to the woods. not stayed
in nature. not left the country. not lived.

the earth called, i answered.
safety is a myth, the mountains know
& my body vibrates:

where am i from? i ask the mountains.
you are a daughter, they say. you are
our daughter.

daughter of ████████████████
daughter of ████████████████
daughter of ████████████████
daughter of ████████████████
daughter of ████████████████
daughter of ████████████████
daughter of ████████████████
daughter of ████████████████

when my parents died █████████████
when my parents died █████████████
when my parents died █████████████
when my parents died █████████████
when my parents died █████████████

[museum]

my great-grandmother's head hangs
in a glass box pedestaling the hall, open lips

embalmed into place. the masks neatly arranged,
heat of her cheeks, still after all these years.

they worshipped rain the guide says, bronze
bodies holding a pot up to the heavens.

what was the prayer to break the sky into tears?
i dig through books & pound my feet.

my land is not my land & it stays dry. in my dreams:
king cobras wrap around my neck. *you've forgotten*

they hiss. & i have. the placard tells me the names
of my people. i pray to a god

& don't know if i pray to the one who is my guard.
yes, it's easy to go mad at the museum

who skinned us to its walls. but what of our brothers
who squandered each gemstone, who tallied the shadows

of their cousins like an abacus? rearranged their beds
to face the west? we justify everything we desire.

i wake & strip the sheets off my bed
the sun already high behind me.

what could it be, this museum of ours? your toes, bare
in the carpet, plush, our ancestors wove by hand
each shape a lullaby they sing to us. a thousand years ago,
your people were the guardians of the rivers. they spoke
in water. mine, the royalty of rock. maybe. i pretend
to be more important than i am. i make up stories
justifying why my voice sounds like sandpaper. how
it smooths. marble makes statue, licks a thigh into a god.
i want so badly to be powerful. then when it comes, i run.
my name on the painting & then i burn down the museum.
the question, always wrong. you can only see as far ahead
as you can see behind. but my life began with death.
on either side, grief-greeted. i stand & wait
for a placard to tell me who i am.

[the women in my family]

their names have been lost

only the winds & only the mountains
keep them. we've forgotten the names

of the mountains, my people, the more
we bent our knees to worship the gods

of the city, the gods with jaguar eyes
who sit in the smog, who could be mistaken

for clouds but for the ink they leave
in our lungs, rorschach paintings doctors

dissect. *what do you see?* my death, certainly
but still no names of the women before

me, or the names of the mountains
& rivers, the promises my ancestors made

to the spirits & then betrayed when they fled,
exchanged land for new land. *what was her*

name? i ask the room of my uncles &
am met with disinterest. *where did she come*

from? & silence. that must be it then:
she came from air. from wind.

from the earth, stilling to quiet. & in
the right moment, when the sun hits

the water, when no one is around,
when i can see the mountains breaking

the sky, i can almost hear them, the women
in my family, the ones who remember their names.

[from]   they lived there for [ ] years before [   ] murdered[1]
              [   ] & had to run. then he, with his [   ] children,[2]
              moved to [   ], but because the tribe they came from

              & the tribe they landed in were at odds, he changed
              their name to [   ] & passed as [   ]. at home
              they knew [   ] but kept it secret

              so quiet, pressed into their marrow. they lost the language.
              they hid the jewelry. their name became another name.
              that's when the forgetting began.

----

1 *the tribal laws were strict,* my cousin says, *hard to follow.*
murder. from my uncle. *no,* an aunt interjects, *not murder, but maybe
attempted.* guessing. covering. obscuring. no one wants the truth.

2 in the official counting, it is only the boys that remain in the stories.
he had [   ] sons before he fled. *but how many daughters?* i ask.
no one knows. *where was his wife from?* his wife was just "his wife."
her name is gone.

the forgetting began earlier. before they were of the [   ]
tribe, when they were of their home. then,
you could walk there. now, a border away. when the
    [   ] empire
came, they decided to convert.[3]

to not appear [   ], they agreed to become
    [   ]. there was god everywhere.

            but they held on to their [   ] & their
    [   ].
until, one day, almost by accident, they didn't. they
    stopped.
then there was nothing from before, they were just
    [   ].

or;

---

3 forced? who can say. in everyone's stories, conversion a joy, a rapture.
eyes of the state everywhere. no one speaks of before. no one would dare.

[nostalgia;]

the cage that keeps my love, a bird
blue-winged & spread over the city. flight
allow me sight, i'm begging to see what was
lost & willing to be seen again. my cards tell
me to surrender, i'm impatient—claim what i
cannot yet have, but here i am, my love
of the past making me long for the places
we've left. you can't unbelong the root, you
see, the trees yawning towards the sky, threaded
to the soil. great mystery of ancestry that wakes
me every night. it's a disease, the past, where i build
my home, i'm waiting on a story that answers
my longing. *why did we become? when did we go?*
well we were ████ & we were ████
& we were ████ until we left, until we—
exhausted, all the fleeing longs
like a blanket hanging on the laundry
by a single clothespin. what were we?
mixed, my cousin says. *not pure.* over-
rated, purity, i rack up a list of new lands
to love, where my daadi walked for pilgrimage
& where they say our eyes come from, the gods
that visit me in my dreams & just watch
my unextraordinary life. oh, i always love
where we left the most, the place that begs

to be remembered. on the bus, i
watch a woman chat to her love on facetime
maurice, she croons. *remember when maurice used
to dress like* & no, stranger i don't remember
maurice or how he used to dress, but i hear
her voice, coated with sugar & i love him,
maurice, all the same.

[my father was not the eldest]

                                though he is rewritten
as so. before him, there were two, girls, nameless.

my grandmother walked to iraq with them, pilgrimage,
one died on the way there. one died on the way back.

buried on the way, in land where borders bloomed
where we cannot go, though, i wouldn't even know

how to find their graves, their names unknown to me
buried decades before i took my first breath. my father

became & was crowned eldest. years later, a younger
brother was born, a baby, sixteen when he crossed

the street & was hit by—what took him doesn't matter.
just that he was taken. & when gone, shattered

my grandfather's heart. the loss of him
blocking the sun. *he never was the same*, they say.

my uncle's grave, sprawling with calligraphy, handwritten
by my grandfather, three marble plaques

holding his grief, his baby son gone & his heart
broken open. my grandfather, writing

out his love in the cleanest way he knew.
to be loved. to be visited. to be marked.

my grandfather's two girls wind now,
rippling the roses at their brother's rest.

[other life]

hair poufed, face round & young in a way that secrets
her age, a sparkly glass of coke on the table.
once, as babies, we danced at the same wedding.
only i rode in the car & she stayed, on her mom's lap.
she grew where i wanted, speaks my father's language.
the branches from the trees turn in on themselves.
growth is in the eye of the beholder, what stays
rooted & what left, kismet, my family says
kismet. instead of karma, what ruled the faith they fled.
i bought ▮▮▮▮▮▮, *don't tell.* she makes me promise.
for her i will keep anything safe. her abundance
a whisper between us, cloaked, our own family
grasping for what a daughter can't be allowed.
i see her, my other life, my mirror.

i see her, my other life, my mirror
grasping for what a daughter can't be allowed
a whisper between us, cloaked from our own family.
for her i will keep anything safe. her abundance
i bought ▮▮▮▮▮▮, *don't tell.* she makes me promise.
kismet. instead of karma, what ruled the faith they fled
rooted & what left, kismet, my family says
growth is in the eye of the beholder, what stays
the branches from the trees turn in on themselves.
she grew where i wanted, speaks my father's language.

only i rode in the car & she stayed, on her mom's lap.
once, as babies, we danced at the same wedding.
her age, a sparkly glass of coke on the table.
hair poufed, face round & young in a way, a secret.

[apus]

in a valley in peru, the apus speak in stone, in boulder, in small blades of grass. their words crawl, a slow rumble, something reaching from below. i am sitting, listening to them, while everyone else around me dances. my friends come to me, concerned that i am not participating. i am [not/not] participating. the apus are talking. i've turned my ear just enough to listen. if i move the wrong way, i   might   never   hear   them   again.

do you understand how precious an angle is? the apus steam & green, junglelush. ancient-faced, dips for eyes. big cat, watching. in my lineage—jinn. but i'm not in my lineage, on my soil. *there is a message, from the mountains of kashmir,* the apus of peru say. it takes ten minutes for them to get this sentence to me. i am unbothered at the wait. mountains speak their own time; their own code. the thrones of my ancestors have sent a message. *even if you can't go, they know you. the fire growls the stones. you are claimed.* the gnats gather. someone's feet dance in ash.

[this is not a metaphor]
[i am not mad]

[despite what you think]
[once]

[the mountains spoke to me]
[once]

[they told me i was theirs]

[archive]

can i imagine myself there, into their family
photos, the archive i could've been in

if i grew where he grew, if my dad stayed
alive. myself right there, alight

in my phuppo's lap, saraiki tongued.
& there again, on the family trip

to the snake-king forest, being scolded
by my chacha for trying to jump off the rocks.

huddled in my grandmother's room, as she told
jinn stories, my face frozen in fear.

there again, at my cousin's wedding, secret
tucked in my dimple, slow dancing with the moon.

& there, on the floor of the kitchen, holding
someone's baby, kohl-eyed & crooning.

what was, was & what could be lives in my mind.
unhealthy, i suppose, to conjure this way, but

i've been photo-less for so long, dreaming
of an archive where i belonged. my years

craning over the same three photos of my dad
& six of my mom. in one,

she's dressed in a blue sari, calling back home,
cradling a phone to her ear.

[after thirty years]

when i return to where
my father was buried i
meet her, his sister, kissed
with rose, hands sliding
into mine at the airport.
they belong there, they already
know how to fit.

they look pakistani, she says
about my partner & they don't

but i know what she means—
they're mine, & so, they're hers, too.

your daadi had rings like yours
in her nose, my mother. one on

either side, one in the middle.
rings all up her ears too.

i fretted for months
over the stars
in my face, wondering
if she would approve. me, thinking
i charted my own life,

my own face, when my daadi
was the blueprint
the whole time.

[the truth is]

                my people only count the men
the truth is half a family tree is a lie
the truth is a poem of a family is a lie

                everyone tells the story different

whoever is loudest wins the memory

the truth is my blood knows something is amiss

         my cards tell me to return to god

the truth is the name for him in my language is not the one i say
the truth is i've been on my knees for many

        the mountains told me where i'm from

the truth is i know how many people would say i'm crazy
the truth is i've spent my life pretending not to be
the truth is even my ancestors were lost
the truth is the ancestors who come to me are the courtesans
the truth is the ancestors who come to me liked to fuck
the truth is the ancestors who come to me were the warriors
        not warriors of light or some fairy shit

          they killed
they were killed

the truth is they left & prayed & wanted
the truth is the mountains speak slowly
the truth is the mountains told me it was okay

                desire bloomed in my belly like an apricot
i lost my freedom

the truth is i loved in secret
the truth is i kept myself hidden
the truth is she strangled me & i screamed
the truth is i liked it

              i'd do it again

the truth is i see them for what they are
those who came before, birthed

me from sky & then left. the warriors
& the ones who fled.

the truth is i see their want & their lost
parts, their fear & heartbreak

flawed, like me, petty. cussing a bitch
out in the street & then

offering zakat. i see them not through what
i want—the better story, neat, proof

of their good, what worthies their lives.
but them: people who peopled,

the ones who loved another but couldn't
the ones who stormed the battle

filled with greed & the ones who stayed home
& forwent the fight, i see them

i try

[he made a movie. it was a flop.]

my aunt says of my dad, betel

leaf in her teeth, chewing in
the back seat, on my way

to the airport, not enough
time to investigate. years later,

she can't remember the plot.
only that it didn't work, only

that he prayed & prayed
it would, only they all laughed

& still laugh now, him desperate
& in costume, only

that my forehead
is pressed to the ground now

doing the same, following
the flopping of my ancestors,

a line of duds, the dreams of my dead,
everyone's names in lights.

[to the god of the city]

i gift my collarbones, the skirt
ending just under my thighs

i gift my throat
hazy with smog, pink & tender.
to the god of the smog i gift

my hand, tight, pen. *what is not*
on my body is not of my body the book
teaches, but truth is i don't know

what my body is made of, silver
littering my wrists, what lives
in my lungs, what managed

to fester there. jaguar-eyed
& prowling, i offer the god
of the city grass & then puke

promptly, rejected. beautiful
& angry, dangerous in a way
i hope to be. a thousand

gray puppets dance
eyes to the sky, broken
by scaffolding. & here i am

looking at my strings, between
knowing they are there &
pretending i don't see.

the line of those who came
before, offering & offering.
trying to get closer. & me

born of the city, pollution
in my hair, scrubbing it
in seawater. the city god

asks for my village & i have
none, only my wanting & even
that, i'm not ready to give

[when i say:]

	[the colonizers took my land]
what i mean is:	[by force, they took me from my rivers]

when i say: [the colonizers took my land]
what i mean is: [the mountains knew me
                      then i was gone]

when i say: [i am landless]
what i mean is: [the orchards of my grandfathers are burned
                      i will never know the sweet taste of their apples]

when i say: [i am an orphan]
what i mean is: [my parents are dead
                      i do not know the shape of their mouths
                      biting into fruit]

when i say: [the colonizers took my land]
what i mean is: [they broke the oaths of my ancestors]
                      [the promises they made to the rivers]
                      [& to the forests]
                      [the snakes are dead & in my spine]

when i say: [orphaning took my land]
what i mean is: [this country runs on who you come from]
                      [child of [   ], child of [   ]]
                      [without a name, no one will call you]

[without a name, you are flower]
[you are markhor]
[flora & fauna]

when i say: [i am an orphan]
what i mean is: [they cut me down for their home]
                         [like the forest, they forgot my name]

when i say: [orphaning took my land]
what i mean is: [my baba had a village]
                         [i do not]
                         [my baba had a baba-tongue]
                         [i do not]

when i say: [i returned]
what i mean is: [the farmer let me eat guavas from his field]
                         [he laughed at how fast i ate them]
                         [i devoured the seeds]
                         [i let them bloom in me]
                         [my american stomach got sick]
                         [the fruit wasn't washed with bottled water]

when i say: [the colonizers took my land]
what i mean is: [by force, my root broke]
                         [i sat for years in its shadow]
                         [i prayed for a way out]

when i say: [i returned]
what i mean is: [the river was littered with plastic]
                         [the forest had been renamed]
                         [my knees turned to snow]
                         [the sun god birthed my eye]

when i say: [i returned]
what i mean is: [the white woman told me, in pakistan
                     the veil is thin
                     between the unseen & the seen]
                     [be careful]
                     [you have to know what you're looking for]
                     [she told me to follow the man from jordan]
                     [or else]
                     [madness]

when i say: [the colonizers took my land]
what i mean is: [i was lost]
                     [in my hand]
                     [their map]

when i say: [the colonizers took my land]
what i mean is: [madness]

when i say: [i returned]
what i mean is: [madness]

when i say: [madness]
what i mean is:

[madness]

a land cleaved from her mother   neighbors who loved

neighbors before killing them   a train of blood   talwaar

& kirpan   the sikh gurdwara burned   cleaved as in

ripped apart   as in a body stretched & ragged   unnatural

teeth tingling   the ghost of your soul always following

children playing soccer in sand   behind them, the buddha

sculpture   torn down   an outline   of what was

the outline   as big as a mountain   the children play

in the shadow of a forgotten   prophet   my father knew

all his hindu neighbors   when they left they gave

my grandmother their plates   asked her to keep them

safe   for years she did   waiting   until she realized

they were never coming back   when my mom died

my father's sister   in a land across the world kept her

wedding dress for us   her girls   waiting for when we'd return

in their graves   my ancestors roll their eyes   when i cry

about colonization   what was lost   *what about*

what we left   for you? the broken buddha   still a buddha

by his outline   the children still play   in his shadow

what can't be erased   even when   it is erased   what

neighbor still remembers   my name   what village

soil-ed my grandmother & sprouted her   what river bows

to man   what birds sing the anthem   my song is older

than a nation   my people lived   longer than the flag   & walked

through mountain & tribe & river & sand   they moved like silk

like snake   they watered   they buried   they waited they lost

they fell   they ran   they new-ed   they bloomed   they grew

[village boy]

the village never left him my aunt says of my dad, village
boy even when he left for new york. 30 years later, the village

still calls when i come, asking what i'm doing each day. my dad
apple-crisp & young, companied by the stars, walking the village.

here, in america, the city dots my dreams. skylines. what i know
best, a subway & deli. my friends listen to podcasts about village

life, our diseases sprouting from how far we moved from the fields.
i stay lusting after what is not mine, but might've been, my baba-village

on my baba-tongue, five knots, the story of four brothers
& a father who built it after fleeing. when my baba left, the village

celebrated the one who traveled to america. the one who dreamed
& walked the dream. the one who died, three girls in new york, village

-less. what years went by, where i dreamed of being belonged, looked
in the mirror & saw a stranger, only to come back & see a village

of my faces, returned? oh, belonging. as gentle as an aunt who knows
a story of the one who made me. oh, belonging, as sweet as the village

built by a river, everyone knowing your name, the stories of your people
the grass & cows & date trees. oh land, never leave me. please. village

me, spirits, the ones i only know from my poems, the ones who cradled
my dad into death. the jinn who guard the land & the people, village

-born. oh, to be held like this. to know the curves of the trees & when
the oranges come. the earth, your earth, your ancestors' earth, village

of me & mine, how i prayed for you, how i longed to know your name
the loss of my father's death shadowing everything, redacting a village

& my belonging, his siblings. their prayers for me, echoing mine for them.
to think i was lost. to be found. i spent my life wanting & there it was:
    my village.

[alhamdulillah, i am belonged]

i step off the plane & you are there
my father's ears on all your heads
doting on me like you last saw
me yesterday, a child crooning
into your arms. i waited years
moving from land to land, dua-ing
for you & you are here, now.
alhamdulillah. you take me like
i am yours, no time lost, thirty
years of scattering unnamed
by your look, by the trees that loop
towards my body, by the sky
filled with smog & falcons.

ii. daughter of [hope]

[somewhere, somewhere, someone]

somewhere, a legion of grandmothers
pray & the empire collapses. somewhere
an aunt digs a circle & buries a secret.

somewhere, a saint's body births
a tree. somewhere, the jinn sit in
the banyans & watch. somewhere,

the planets dance & everyone's birth
chart tightens. embers in the chest.
somewhere, the fish carry

the prayers to god. somewhere, an
ancestor speaks in a dream. somewhere,
the ICE truck gets towed before the raid.

under the rubble a grandfather reaches
his hand to the sky. under the rubble,
400,000 hearts, slowing. somewhere,

a prime minister says *violation of international
law* & no government does anything.
the government kidnaps its own people.

somewhere, someone cries for help &
something else answers. somewhere,
an elder's wrinkled hands sew a blanket

for a child. somewhere, someone touches
a tasbeeh. somewhere, someone lights a candle
at their altar. the plantation burns

& water refuses to give its gift.
something else answers. someone pulls
the tower. somewhere, someone survives

under the rubble, someone's hand opens,
someone's fist pulses, someone stays alive.

[i don't know what will kill us first:
the race war or what we've done to this earth]

so i count my hopes: the bumblebees
are making a comeback, one snug tight
in a purple flower i pass to get to you;

your favorite color is purple but Prince's
was orange & we both find this hard to believe.
today the park is green, we take grass for granted

the leaves chuckle around us; behind
your head a butterfly rests on a tree; it's perched
there for our entire conversation; by my old apartment

was a butterfly sanctuary where i would read
& two little girls sat next to me; you caught
a butterfly once but didn't know what to feed it

so you trapped it in a jar & gave it to a girl
you liked. i asked if it died. you say you like
to think it lived a long life. yes, it lived a long life.

it lived a long life.

[the ocean's tryna fuck]

when i come to her i try to stay thigh-deep.
the ocean, her mouth running just under my ass

until she waves, reaches up & slaps
me in the face. fist full of salt-soaked

flowers i offered her—
she pushes me to my knees & drags me

& i go, sand-stained, wherever she pulls,
bussing it wide open for her.

she's so frothy, all she does is cream.
when i pull back she spits in my mouth

& me, silly sub that i am, fall
in love at her rough & gentle, at her tender

throne. what a miracle, to have a body
so i can meet her like this, her salt brimming

my skin. & later, when i'm miles away
i bend & she spills out my ears

my nose, my dress soaked with her

[smell is the last memory to go]

but on my block, citrus &
jasmine trees knock

me back into the arms of my dead
mother. i ask ross *how can a tree*

be both jasmine & orange, on my block
my neighbors put up gates & stare

they don't like to share, on my block
a tree i can't see, but can smell,

a tree that can't be both but is.
on my block, my mother's skirt twirls

& i inhale her ghost, perfume
on my block, a fallen orange

smashed into sidewalk
its blood pulped on asphalt,

jordan hands me a jasmine
& by the time i get home

all its petals are gone

[orange]

my days with you fill with new knowing;
the crumbs that gather on the right side
of your mustache, waiting to be licked.

your fingernails, jagged
little cliffs that gather dirt & paint
& easily, they find your earlobe

when you need comfort & a moment
of quiet. you, in a shalwar kameez
pointing out the couples you think

are married out of love or arranged
by elders, like how my uncle, befuddled,
asked me, *so you would rather marry a stranger*

than someone i know when i told him
about you, sitting in the other room
playing with our dog, whose feet smell

like fritos & who pretends he can't walk
up the stairs just so i'll carry him.
there were years i went without it—knowing.

the months we spent in quarantine
& i watched tiktok videos of couples
approximating for myself the curve of love:

the inside of someone's hand, the shower
water gathering in the dip of your back. oh Allah,
give me the gift of knowing, of knowing you

of walking the land of my father. his siblings,
their love of seviyan, like my baba's. & my baba's
brother telling me the story of my father

eating orange after orange from the village
until the whole basket was gone & how
confused he was, my baba, wondering

who had eaten them all. oh, to know. the years
after my father died stretching into more years.
i forgot his face & searched my dreams

for any sign of him. & now, in his country,
in his home, in front of his brother. my father's
face on another. how long

i've wanted to know & now, the knowing
surrounds me. & you, the one
i love, sitting next to me as my family pours

from another language, story after story. my phuppo
looking at albums with you, rambling in urdu
as though you know, as though it's yours.

kinu, you say, turning to me. *kinu means orange.*

[poor you, you orphan]

my partner says
when i ask them
for the tenth
time if my family
is annoying
or too much
after thirty years
of being lost
from each other
& they laugh
this is what family is

this is what family
is,

mountains watching
across the city &
my family crowding
our apartment
with medicine packets
even though i said no.
but i can't say no
to their smiles
& concern, no matter
how many books

on boundaries i read
this is what family is:

ushering us too
close through the market
afraid we'd get lost
even though
we're grown &
demanding
we eat halwa
every morning
with them
before our day
begins just so
they can say
hello

[in the country where hugs are banned]

there are still birthdays & today
is yours, bright thing, sun aglow

through every blind of my window
& i know this day the rays were made
for you & even the breeze seems

to mouth your name, a gift
to the earth & it's unfair that today
of all days, the whole country is grounded

we are not allowed out, not allowed to gather
in your bright & instead click the link sent
to each of us, our faces crowding the screen

each in our separate worlds
each with our own suns & breezes & names
in our own countries of couch cushions & lampshades

our own countries of plants & post-it notes
in our own countries of touches & it seems
impossible to draw a line down the hall

on any given day, but especially this one,
cruel even, this new world where everyone
is their own kingdom & the riot cops stand at

arms, ready to fire at the slightest touch, so
even though it is not allowed, even though
we could get in trouble, i—

[i won't forget]

my father: sideburns down the length of his face my age now & ripe
my age now & alive his husky voice's crackle like the night's wind
through corn, fields of bell-bottoms, fields of pomade, my mother's
oversized sunglasses crowded on her face crowded in the only
english movie theater that plays amitabh bachchan my mother
watching the blown-out screen, the smoke spilling from light, how
he is able to be in all places at once, all the places she can't be, the
man on the screen a kind of god maybe, my grief, a kind of god
maybe—in all places all at once, replaying their every story, a kind of
god maybe: my father's nazar, his long look, his luck-laced lungs,
breathing my mom's hands as they whisper next to each other in the
theater, the almost touch, blood electric, my father watching her,
his sideways glance on her thick eyelashes, my father's stomach
blinks & blinks & a thousand manoj kumars blink his insides,
his heart pumps *main na bhoolunga* on beat, *main na bhoolunga*
in chorus, *main na bhoolunga* the theater singing, my mother's
fingers on his palm & maybe this is what falling in love is like: a
handsome man jumbling your intestines, a handsome man belting
the song & you, afraid to blink in case it was smoke this whole time.

[he was chaotic]

my teacher says
of their cat, now gone

missing. in his absence
everything is still.

the small, silvered line
in a grief-filled night.

when my love arrived into my life
they brought noise. their ideas,

their laugh, their loud joy. they rumbled
thunder in the distance.

then, the dog came too. bark & growl.
his fluffy-eared need to play.

before, it had been so quiet. minutes
looming to more minutes.

time. oh, time. they came
& the seconds collapsed.

entire months, blurred. love,
a time machine. love, an ocean-bellied

mystery. on the morning i watch
dolphins play in pairs, my teacher

tells me again about their cat. oceans
in their eyes. the dolphins play

with each other. they flirt. one day,
when my loves leave, be it by choice—

theirs, mine, or Allah's—sadness
threatens to take. but today,

when the dolphins leave mine
& my teacher's sight, the water is quiet.

still, under the sun.

[on the plane]

you don't say you miss me.
just—if the apocalypse

comes, i'm the farthest point
in the world from you. how

would you get to me?
the line disconnects.

dramatic. we're already so far
into the apocalypse, worrying

about it is redundant. to you,
the one i love, our tiktok

dms serve proof of life—
the fluffy kitten, constipated,

who strains in the litter box;
the boy swimming in his timbs

joins the brawl for his elder;
a cooking video i will never

make but convince myself
i will; a south asian actress

tumbling down three flights of stairs
into a suitcase; the broken crocs

clawing like alligators, still on someone's
feet; small tiny joys i collect

for when i miss you & when i don't
hear from you, send

annoyingly, instead of saying
i'm here. at the end

i find you.

[i can't fight]

but for you i would

gladly get my ass kicked
to prove a point

the point being
my imagination gets away

from me most times
& the rare day i make

my way to the gym
& put my headphones on

& let myself dream
my weird dream thoughts

i become the star
of an action movie

no one wants to see,
where someone scuffs your shoe

& i rain my fists bloody
where some idiot scuffs your heart

& i cartwheel over three lanes
of traffic to save your honor

i burn down entire villages
of people who looked at you

the wrong way
the point being

my love for you
makes me a warrior

of a losing army,
the point being my love

could turn my body
into a punching bag, my love

you turn my body
into a whistle, into a red light

& i beg for more
do you understand

what i'm saying—i would pain
for you, gladly, even when you didn't,

even when you would never ask.

[february in lahore]
          for zainab & fareed

we're married now, zainab says, leaning over another
guest at the dholki, *your ideas are my ideas.* oh, to love another

so much their thoughts become your own. to look with love
at your love & think, this too can be mine, this beauty here, another

bright bird, paradise, planted in the garden of your heart.
fareed was taking credit you see, for inviting her friends out. another

sweet way of joining, her friends as his, him, sitting there,
looking gently at who she loves, welcoming another & another

& what is marriage, but a world built together? but a joining
of cloth, of weaving a delicate thread so closely against another

they fit through the same needle. what keeps your heart soft?
the hawks flying over lahore like pigeons, a man cutting another

man's hair outside at the makeshift barbershop, the layers
of petals pressing against the soil at the grave. another

day breaking open, the sun spilling across the sky, your forehead
pressing into the earth during sujood, your sister's eyes on another's

face. these loves that bloom more love, the heart petaling open
into a river of tulips. oh, Allah, bring me to them, another

one i can love for a little while longer, in this world where
they bomb, where they gun, where they end, where another

child is called a martyr & those that could stop it looked away.
in this world where we're taught to fear, to flee, to fight another

at the end, i want nothing more than you—an other,
you, another moment, another who i chose, another

who i walk with. fill my cup with another.
& when that's done, another, again.

[they're in their lord of the flies bag]

terence says about the boys nestled
in the mouth of the waterfall

the one boy's eyes opened to the sky, legs
wrapped around the rock to keep him

alive, afloat, the river running over
him, kissing him just so, his body

an interruption in the water, the rush
& roar of its call partitioned by the fall

dividing it from itself. the other boys
perched around him like water nymphs

staring off beyond the mountains' dip,
where the sun sets. the boys so landed

they become part of the land, the roots rooting
around their ankles. yes, in their lorded fly

bag, but a lord of the flies before
it gets dark. before they do what they do

to piggy, before the split & hunt. wild,
still. boys who jump from as high

as the trees, into the water cradled
so lovingly by rock, boys who ford

the river in their socks, throwing their shoes
to any soft land willing to catch. the water,

a mother: both healing & scolding, both soft
& gathering pressure at the fall. shallow

enough to walk, deep enough to dive, the boys
know her, where to step

& where to not, how to say hello, when
to let her sleep. their big toes scraping

into the moss, curling to hold them steady, fingernails
finding the hook between roots to anchor, to pull

their bodies upwards. the coquís coquíing their song.
the sun winking its set. everything green; nothing

poisoned. alhamdulillah, to know land
so well, you can play with it. to never second-guess

where your foot lands, how to get your body
where it wants to go. to be so fromed, you from.

alhamdulillah, to cradle the fall & not fall.
to hear the river's rush & feel safety. wild.

the boys. in their lord of the flies bag. yes,
the boys, there, on top of the waterfall. pulling

crumbs of leaves out of each other's hair. the boys:
wild, but not lost. the boys, wild & belonged.

[practice]
          for terence & atheel

we would say, *it all comes
down to practice.* let me practice for you
then, love, making a cup of tea, honeyed

just the way you like. let us practice
dreaming, under the convertible's
open sky, the stars morphing

into their own story. all love is an exercise
in practice. in learning how to see what
another opens for you, & once

opened, stays that way. how lucky am i,
to practice loving with you. to watch
your practice, growing, holding us now

scented of amber & oud. what time
brings, what harvest, what gorgeous
bounty of gather & water, what joy

in arriving at your doorstep. oh love,
thank you for the world where
i open my door & find you, where you

open your door & a table of loves wait
ready to celebrate, where the hummingbird
sings & we know its song, where we drive

on the narrow road, at the cliff of the beach
just to get to the stream. where atheel giggles,
we're at the edge of a continent, can you imagine?

awe-soaked, the birds dipping in & out
of view. what a world we live in, thank you
for letting me borrow your eyes to see

how you see, to love how you love,
terence, hand on my shoulder
& promising *i'll come with you*

when i confess the journey that takes me
to the home of my fear. oh, my loves. what i learned
with you was to walk to the edge of the unknown

& thank the wind, bless the earth.
what i learned with you is how to count
the mysteries, how to never ink the story

that's still being written. what i learned
with you was to live a season romancing
a single word: wonder. awe. mystery.

unfolding. like a prayer. always.
the thrill of getting lost in the woods, endless,
what i learned from you was the choice

of love, of watching the cradle of another
& saying yes, this is my practice, this is
where i want to build my home & why.

iii. daughter of [border]

[when we thought the world would end]

i didn't think it would be like this
watching my beloveds through facetime
on the tens of tens of apps downloaded
so i can hear the scattered voices
of everyone i love & the silence
of my apartment building, so loud,
my whole world is now my kitchen
& yellow couch & i haven't touched
anyone in days, my fingers press into
my own body, i surprise myself in the mirror
the meditation says to think of a happy day
i remember being packed in that wooded
house for angel & hieu's graduation
& danez saying *the bitch can't dance*
as i wiggled my flailing body, trying
& how easy it was to hold safia's hand
my knee against shira's in the back of the minivan
to brush the hair out of sam's eyes
as we played ja rule too loud on the way
to weep at our friends graduating the bitch
of an mfa, the years we've all spent
in heartache of a thing we might be good at
the years spent changing cities, moving
farther & farther from our loves because
this might be it. 'might' is a strong word

like *this might be our new lives* & *this might*
be forever, the ellipses of waiting & all
the mights pile up together around my bed
in the morning i have to sift through the mights
to make my day worthwhile, to push my body
into salat, i have to work to not
let the mights get stuck in my chest,
to not drown in their sorrow
& we've spent years preparing for the apocalypse
when the white boys took up torches
& when that idiot got elected & ice continued
to melt, but i never thought it would be like this
us all, islanded, watching each other on screens
& before, when we could hold each other
when we didn't know it would end like this
danez & i promised when the world
was really coming to an end, like truly
coming to an end, we would find
each other in our best dresses, i would maybe
even buy a fur, & we'd ride it out together
& on the phone, we say, *well bitch. this might be it.*

[everyone grieves at the walk light]

its dull blink, we stay green.

necks pivot towards the concrete
gravity pleads all our names.

what would it take to join the earth?
the trees spent thousands of years

conversing with each other, chitchatting
about the jinn in their branches

before we cut them down for our phone lines.
we watch everything through a screen.

even the sun dipping into its sleep.
it's better to remember. & the photo twins

thousands of photos in my phone. i only look
at them when i'm too sad to get out of bed,

which only makes me sadder. back in the time
when we had offices they put in lights

to mimic the sun. like flowers, our bodies
craned towards their warmth. pretending

is better than not. what is lost, is lost.
the hair that used to be there

making an M on your forehead no matter
how much castor oil slathered. the man's face

behind you fades into another's face. once,
in a village, the names of every new birth

were recorded in a log. a family bloomed.
& bloomed again. now, no one knows

the name of your mother. the jinn who used
to live in the trees are houseless, rooting among

blades of grass. i lived in the past tense,
when we all gathered there on the sidewalk.

our body heat, its own village. it was brief.
then it ended. it was brief & i never saw you again.

[nazar]

what's not mine/ back to sender/ an endless
night's sky/ the country my great-great-great-grand left/

the tribe/ silver coins made into jewelry/ crowning the head
the house of my mother

& when she died/ her brothers took/ my dead
dad's money/ blooming

in the account of my uncle/ from the soil on the other
side of the border where my family

lived/ my mom's gold/ passed through the hands
of her sisters/ kept in drawers

& never returned/ an invisible border around me
& my sisters/ orphaned/ evil-eyed

my kin is my wealth/ a basket of ripe apples
orcharding/ except when they lied

& stole/ from me/ a death being the perfect
heist/ like stealing from a baby

& we were/ babies/ my sisters frilly in their dresses
& adult-less/ dead parents/ first betrayal

our creators/ dead/ & the adults left/ thieves/ living
in a world/ where nothing/ enoughed/

of course/ it's on me/ the look/ the eye/ what you
call/ the excuse/ so much misfortune

in the west/ bad luck/ a raw deal/ tragedy/ blah
blah/ blah/ i roll out my janamaz & line my eyes

with black/ i draw daggers with kohl/ tattoo
my skin/ the hand/ i'm named after

& the mirror/ i practice/ *no one can fuck with me/* make
myself/ mine/ make myself tough/ even

the spirits tremble/ my body drips of oil/ i smell
abundant/ a curse/ broken/ an eye

weeps/ a tear falls/ a spring is born/ a whole river
that runs/ & runs/ away

[here we are]

heading into the worst of human light

the camp of burned bodies as the woman celebrates

her new furs, her come-up. children eating grass

a few blocks away, separated by a fence, the adults make

plans to go to drinks & tell tales of their dating escapades,

of friends pregnant & carrying something new. life moving forward,

neighbors overwatering their lawns, new bulbs failing to root.

how much water, to remove the smell of blood? the ocean

sings of bodies. they mermaid the deep sea. on the other

side of the fence, they complain about the crops this year.

they stab the tree, then wear its fruit. what grows here?

atop the cemetery of the living? people are being lost every day.

look what i just did, sugar-sweetened the word. murdered.

people are being murdered every day. online, people fight

about the right language to be used. *do you condemn? do you condemn?*

i can't condemn what i haven't lived. my parents died,

tragic, yes, but not murdered. i live with my orphaning every day.

& now, there are blocks after blocks of eliminated parents. what

do those children do with their dead? with their grief?

condemn what? the boy who watches his little

brother shaking after the bomb blows the street? who does he grow

up to be? oh, allah. cover them. in gaza, mothers write their children's

names on their arms. a baby girl smaller than her name can fit.

what's worse, what's worse than this?

[on the eve of ramadan]

they murder cities of people in palestine & sudan
the videos broadcasted to our phones, a father
carrying his murdered child in plastic bags & misfired aid
parachutes murder more. flocks of beautiful children,
ribbons in their braids, waving white flags, gone. what language
can i use, what language left. above, a kite flies in the sky,
untethered. below, a body lies slaughtered. there's an internet
blackout & then, an entire neighborhood, gone. sorry
for being redundant. sorry for not having more
beautiful words to make you care. i don't know
how to write this, other than plainly.

in america, they celebrate an award show & applaud
themselves for diversity, for how far they've come.
my friends prepare to fast. my friends: my language
has run out. all around me, kids are dying & healers
in the west talk about karma, debts owed. what is the god
you pray to, that turns their back to this?

depression is not an adequate feeling. more like, there is a well
of grief in me so deep, if i stand on the edge of it i might
go mad. there are millions, standing at the edge of their hearts
screaming into the night's sky. i keep repeating myself. the award
show gets standing ovations. my non-muslim friends text cheery
ramadan mubarak texts. the ummah fast & there are bodies, broken

under rubble, waiting to be found. the war that is not a war
but a genocide has been going for [   ] years. it didn't start
when they say it did. someone drew a border not his.
signed a paper. denied who was there. who had always
been there. make no mistake. that's what started this.

[point towards the beauty]

the poem says.
where? what gentleness?

the little boy guiding
his brother

to say *there is no god*
but god, with his last breath

the man dressed as mickey
mouse for the kids

whose houses are destroyed
by bombs. a mom

scouring for ingredients
to make her five-year-old

a birthday cupcake.
a soft candle celebrating his day:

i don't have cake, but i have
my books, the man says,

surrounded by pages.
a land of pages, endless.

in indian-occupied kashmir, there are mass graves of an estimated
8,000–10,000 unidentified men & boys, dragged from their homes &
never seen again. despite photos documenting their lives, the army
denies these men ever existed.

i.

when the army comes, the men disappear

when their wives ask where the men went

they are told the men did not exist.

the men never existed. they imagined

their husbands, slippers neat by the front

door, entire afternoons spent with a ghost

by the river, the roti tucked in the basket.

weddings, fantasied by entire villages. after,

the women walk the soil, barefoot, searching

for a stone that might tell them where

their husband lay. they speak in the language

of land, their grief held by the mushrooms,

by each tiny blade of grass & dancing pollen,

fragile. once, you loved me & then you were taken.

ii.

oh beloved/ let me follow you/ let me lay

roses where you rest/ let me write your

epitaph in the dirt/ soft/ in case you return/

did you flee to the trees/ did you cross

a border/ did you forget/ was it painful/

were you afraid/ could you find peace/ is it light

where you are now/ can you smell the jasmines/

did you run/ was someone next to you/

did they hold your hand/ were you in prison/

did they beat you/ did you break/ was it by gun/

did they turn you around/ did you say my name/

did you close your eyes/ were you brave/

does it matter/

iii.

the army does not speak to the earth.

they crack it open, metal & drill.

dirt holds the bodies of the men,

of the ghosts, the earth blooms

their names through wildflowers, multicolored

& frail. there was no man. only the story

of him. here, the men disappear. here,

the women marry their imagination,

their children: miracles, a ghost story survived.

their children: dancing in the night's light.

their children: staring into the woods.

their children: half whisper & half birdsong.

[ya latif, ya latif, ya latif]

chanted so fast my jaw numbs.

in the back of the masjid, the speaker
goes & i can only hear the hum, the words

lightning so fast they become another
word entirely. the stone in me waters.

i river. frantic & hairy i go to my waxer before
my flight. *the girls nah work today,* the woman

says, resigned to her chair, beady eyes
to the window. she points me to a shop

i've never been, too pink & bright. ICE
trucks stop at every corner. orange

man's fear, spittle at the podium
& everyone scatters in the daylight.

one week into his re-rule & the photos
come: guantánamo, men picked from

neighborhoods like fruit, shirtless
& tattooed, pressed beside each other.

neck crooked against neck, gentle. hiding
their faces from the camera's look.

ya latif, ya latif, ya latif. what kindness:
hands bound & unclothed & still,

shielding each other with their bodies.
tender. too tender. what is ours to look?

what is not? i couldn't hold the gentle. intrusion.
i carry them in my river. i chant ya latif,

ya latif, ya latif for each one in the photo,
for each one not in the photo.

at the pink shop down the street, still
no girls—just the owner papered

& safe. a gen z-er argues with her too
long about a misplaced eyebrow hair. they stand

side by side, looking in the mirror
for ten minutes. *every time i come here, you*

do this, the gen z-er huffs, then leaves. the block
hot, the trucks move & she might text

a friend *i'm never coming here again.* i let
the couple with the newborn go before

me. *how old?* the owner croons. *three weeks.*
i watch the owner, thread between her teeth

her neck gentle, un-necked by others, bobbing,
back & forth, its own dhikr in the waxing shop,

its tender metronome;
ya latif/ ya latif/ ya latif/ ya latif

[freedom song]

what does it mean, to be free? i sip coke at my phuppo's, azaadi
on the walls of the university, free kashmir sprawled, azaadi

on my body. when i walk the streets of lahore men stare.
can i write the poem that makes me free, that brings azaadi

to my lips? i say i want to drink from its waters, but i know
what it means to be human & dumb, to pray & when azaadi

comes to shun, to judge & say not like this. control, a bitch
deeply un-free, that sticks me in my own mind, azaadi

i plead, come help free me from me. what an overworked god
the policeman's gun turning towards the sand, the ocean's azaadi

crashing blue wave after blue into the fishing boat, thieving
life from its water. everything is a freedom song, i hear azaadi

in the wind & in the flood, in the sparkle of the sun on a child's
arm. it calls to me. & i turn my back when azaadi

isn't convenient. in my bed, i dream of a baby with my love's
face & my fingers, biologically impossible. *azaadi*

could be a good name for a kid, i muse, us gays dreaming farther
into the future than we're allowed. our pretend kid, azaadi

in a way that dances like a ghost at the edge of my dream.
i'm a shadow girl, born to someone else's longing. azaadi

please, my grandfather made his boys promise not to return
to kashmir until it's free, our house ours again & azaadi

tolled in the street. we've been waiting a long time. return. our
right. they say. maybe. it slips. water through my fingers. azaadi.

what's a dream & what's awake? everything a maze & another maze.
& you, pray a way. in the poems, on your lips, to every god: azaadi.

[still life, interrupted by border]

    i.   what is is not what always was

when [BORDER] we drive past [BORDER] the mountains that [BORDER] after the dragon-king. [BORDER] litter our path, descended from the lion-headed serpent, just a [BORDER] now. what [BORDER]. what meets us now [BORDER]s what could've been. my [BORDER], dead, guides the way. her mother, also [BORDER], shows [BORDER]. [BORDER] is just [BORDER] & not a constant throb that ticks my waking hours. what makes [BORDER]? some mathematical equation of geography, language & [BORDER], what one ancestor [BORDER] & what one [BORDER]. who was [BORDER] & who was forgotten. the mountain grass silks, lightly speckled with snow. patoos draped on the [BORDER]s of men, khol [BORDER]ing their eyelids. sandalwood, badaam & ghee; the spell that keeps the spirits at bay. we walk, the same [BORDER] my grandmother & grandfather did, [BORDER] in tow. honestly, there were probably more. i don't always [BORDER] their names. allah, [BORDER] me. i'm a terrible study. no [BORDER] wants me. in the time before [BORDER]. when the water spirits held the lake, when the mountain spirits sat on their hinds, my friend tells me her [BORDER] used to drive from [BORDER] to [BORDER], hatchback, [BORDER] tied to the [BORDER].

ii.   what was lost, what wants

[BORDER] [BORDER]
[BORDER] [BORDER]
[BORDER]
[BORDER] [BORDER]
[BORDER]
[BORDER] [BORDER] [BORDER] [BORDER]
[BORDER]
[BORDER],
[BORDER] [BORDER]
[BORDER]
[BORDER]
[BORDER]
[BORDER]
[BORDER]
[BORDER]
[BORDER] [BORDER]
[BORDER]

[BORDER] [BORDER] [BORDER]
[BORDER] [BORDER]

iii.   what was & could be, again

when i go, finally we drive past the main city into the mountains that are named after the dragon-king. snakes litter our path, descended from the lion-headed serpent, just a legend now. what was, was. what meets us now whispers what could've been. my mom, dead, guides the way. her mother, also dead, shows us the line we cross. kashmir is just kashmir & not a constant throb that ticks my waking hours. what makes identity? some mathematical equation of geography, language & tribe, what one ancestor chose & what one left. who was loudest & who was forgotten. the mountain grass silks, lightly speckled with snow. patoos draped on the shoulders of men, kohl lidding their eyelids. sandalwood, badaam & ghee; the spell that keeps the spirits at bay. we walk, the same walk my grandmother & grandfather did, eight babies in tow. honestly, there were probably more. i don't always remember their names. allah, forgive me. i'm a terrible study. no religion wants me. in the time before nation. when the water spirits held the lake, when the mountain spirits sat on their hinds, my friend tells me her grandmother used to drive from england to pakistan, hatchback, luggage tied to the top of the car.

iv. daughter of [pain]

i thought i thought i thought i thought i thought
i thought i thought i thought i thought i thought
i thought i thought i thought i thought i thought
i thought i thought i thought i thought i thought
i thought i thought i thought i thought i thought
i thought i thought i thought i thought i thought
i thought i thought i thought i thought i thought
i thought i thought i thought i thought i thought
i thought i thought i thought i thought i thought
i thought i thought i thought i thought i thought
i thought i thought i thought i thought i thought
i thought i thought i thought i thought i thought

                                        i was wrong

[no one can take my anger]

not even you who caused it.

& no one can take my madness
not even my honeyed friends

who try to pull me back from
the edge of myself, who update

each other in the groupchat
of how my body is wasting

how i've stopped eating,
frail, my withering wrists.

no one can take my vengeance,
not the healer sent to fix

my spine or the flame i confess
to in the dark of the day.

no one can take my mundane
memories, us trying to fit

three suitcases in the back
of an uber, everyone mad

at the american way we take
up space. & us in the doctor's

office in the sticky heat, your skin
slightly gray from dengue &

the doctor's voice: *yes, it feels like*
you're going to die. like every bone

is broken. the good thing is,
you won't. die. it's only a feeling.

the bad thing is, there's no medicine.
i followed the shopkeeper

to cut the leaves off a plant
out back & brew you a tea.

temporary relief. medicine, no.
magic, no. but relief, small,

while you slept & i waited
on the porch, trying to figure out

what to do. no one can take
my soft heart, unblocking you

when she leaves, worried you
might be unwell. there is a story

mundane & unfinished. i loved
the wrong person. or, i loved

the right person & it wasn't
enough. i loved & then betrayal

sank its teeth. i loved & then
bled, for too long after. i picked

the scab & bled some more.
my bleeding meant i was still

yours, somehow. child
of loss. broken & left

by those who claimed to love
me, still looking for hope.

all artists are the children of loss,
my teacher says. all artists call

to betrayal & make a new world
in the bruise.

[fennel seed]

hidden in the bra
i don't wear, to become
something new. & so,
the fennel runs down
my stomach, sticking, sweat,
sheer determination.

always a wife, i stick to you
even when you're with her
& i'm in another country. a pub
i think you would like, the sun
dipping over a green i want
to share with you. love

is madness, how small i promise
to make myself, just to stay
with you. i threaten to move
out of its orbit & you take her
on a road trip. my body is not
a body, but a ghost. i haunt

& wail. a thing made from horror.
a thing they might one day write
a movie about. a thing dusted
& torn, in pain, begging to be seen.
but no one looks up from their drink.

[madness]

i was curious, about who made my friend
feel safe, she says, my friend of six

years, after she fucked you, my partner.
we dreamed for months of a prayer room.

crafted, our altars next to each other
so our ancestors could land safely

& meet. our council of dead, a witness.
what is this dumb

life i built? my love for you sloppy
& too loud. my dead

watch as she talks, shifting & side-eye.
your fingers reaching for hers, your eyes

adoring, drinking the word. *safety.*
my own falling, falling loudly

from under me, a fish plucked
from the ocean, breathing on the dining

table, my one open eye on you.

un-wifed & orphaned.
daughter of who?

you whispered a promise
& it clung to my finger, a ring.

[opposite of midas]

what i touch leaves
me, dirt.

what i love has its own
life & makes plans
without me. what i love

cheats. at the blackjack
table, drunk. what i love
has teeth that glint.

[other life]

there is a version of me, still
with you. frolicking

in london, gathering flowers
both annoyed & in love

with the land of my colonizers
picking the right cut

of salmon at the market
to surprise you

while you work—
smell of salt, lemon

zest, bright
pink meat, firm.

[when you told me about her]

i brought you
to the park & fucked a tree.
you watched
me coat its bark
with my cum, jealous.

love is madness
& i'm too woo-woo
for my own good.
in my dreams, my tree
calls my name
in a language only it speaks

full of seed & root
leaves dripping with rain
& flashing in my mind.
i think this is the best
sex i've ever had
the branches holding me

sturdy & tough. *all of nature
bends to love you,* says
my friend, *my sweet bb
it was always in your character*

arc to fall in love with a sap
claims another. nature

is coming. & cumming
again. dizzy with touch.
my mind, dizzy with wood.
my feet, pressed into mud.
molasses-thick, down my skin.

[cursed]

point one finger
& three turn back to you
the saying goes, so i'll

point my whole fucking
hand, open-palmed & up
to Allah, like what do you

want me to do with this
little bitch you made? gossip
can be a sin, sure

it can also be a savior
enveloping against the one
who won't let you leave

even when you beg. a thousand
& one aunties, dead, around you
jasmine-scented braids rustling

in the wind. i'm sure there
are men in my family line
who weren't shit.

i know they'd still ride
from out the grave
to save me from my scream.

i'm screaming now, i'm tolling
from every bell tower
i can find. can you hear me?

where you got me fucked up
is i'm not interested in goodness.
the lightning's in my head.

pleasure at my feet.
there are snakes in the water
whose slithering i'll chop

off clean with my fruit fork.
meaning, when you cheated
on me, i dropped to my knees

& thanked god i wasn't you.

[& what a miracle]

                              my tiny, tiny body
the way it cannot fold onto itself
for me to touch my toes, how my thighs

seize up in the yoga class as everyone
else gazelles into downward
dog, alhamdulillah to my ragged breath

how it pulls & bites the air as i waddle
up the long flight of stairs to my beloveds
who laugh inside, who wait

patient as the earth's slow rotation for my body
to arrive & mashallah to the scars that forest
my legs, leftover from mosquito bites scratched

awry, the rolls that crease my back
when i turn to look at the helicopter dip-dancing
in the distance, the sound louder than my knees'

crackle as i bend to tie my undone laces, as i scrape
the plaque from between my teeth with my jagged
nail, my body, my body, all the ways it sings.

[pagamento]

i cursed the frog
that found its way into
my house. murderous, i laid
poison for the ants. i threw
my moon in the trash.
when you fucked her, i wished
you a hall of mirrors.
doomed to endless versions
of yourself. i prayed you'd undo
each other. & you did. i took
from the earth without permission.
unkind, i ate the fruit
before it was ready.
demanded it bend to my time.
the root of the word *evil*—unripe.
the older man touched my body
unripe, before it was ready. i put myself
in a paper bag. i wanted to grow
up quick. i wanted to be ripe.
then, i demanded it all slow down.
i got annoyed at the dog. that fluffy
pouf, just a baby. gone, i miss him
terribly. playing in my hair.
running to the door. a puppy-shaped
hole in my throat. i argued

when i could've listened.
i scoffed when someone confessed
their pain. i cussed out the fire for its roar.
demanded it be watered. thought
i knew better than the earth. me,
small peanut. me, easily crushed & building
a fort in bed, refusing to emerge.
me, too much salt. not enough water.
payment to the spirits. my awful awful.
my rooms of muck, closeted in my body-sack.
the noodles in my mind, worms, eating
the lettuce. me, at the altar of earth,
handing over my catalogue of hurts,
every soft dimple on my skin.

v. daughter of [dirt]

[alhamdulillah i am belonged]
[alhamdulillah i am claimed]
[alhamdulillah i called & the mountains answered]
[alhamdulillah my people still remember my name]

[what existed before?]

i.

believe it or not, there was a me
before you. there, walking the long
grasses of L.A., skirt gathered in hand
stoking the crock-pot, smelling the orange
tree peeking from a neighboring gate.
there i was: falling asleep on my yellow
couch, foot curved & unblanketed, dangling
close to the edge, the rosemary tea getting
cold. me, again, gathering my friends
at the party, giggling too loud, perfect beauties
of white eyeliner & red lips, little disco balls
glittering under the night. there, again: eating
chocolate cake & picking out vegan cheese
at the bougie bodega, poem in my purse.

ii.

me before you: a villager
running alongside the wind, grass
sticking to my foot. in the forest the smoke
heavied, some fell to their knees, some let
the incense carry their call to the heavens,

& some gave their bodies' weight to the earth.
before there was a border, before there
was a military, there was land & those who knew
how to speak to it, & the animals guarding their doors.
we moved when we needed to move, along river,
through grass, slithering like snake. before i knew
the word for *country* i knew myself, the law
of my own body, my earth, my name.

iii.

before the shadow, there was the sun,
surya, carved from clay & rock, hot
& crowned with gemstones. gold, glittering
catching a ray & tossing it back to the sky.
before the shadow there was sangya, among
the clouds, cool & airy, married
to heat. before the shadow, there was the buddha,
mustached & in the alps, pressed into their curves,
chiseled to near-perfect. the gods lay
in the mountains, the gods lay in the rock.
before the shadow: those who bent their knees
to fire, slipped wishes on paper to feed, offered
their dead to the sun to feast. before,
there was. no matter what they say now.

iv.

before i saw myself through your eyes
i saw myself through my own, fumbling,

sure, but there, in the mirror: girl of gold,
boy of quiet, eyes big & opened like a doe.
before, i was cool as the clouds, i closed
my eyes & the rain came, it trickled down
my spine & when i walked by the ocean
she knew me by my river, by the spirits
who stayed with me even when my family
left. my ancestors carved snakes in my back
as a warning. sure, i startled easily,
but there was a sun inside me, i knew
its hours, i knew how to worship,
i knew how to pray.

[what was rewritten?]

i.

a country came &
who was before fled

a border was drawn
& the walls got small

they destroyed the temple
& the sun lost its rest.

the forest asked to be soothed
but no one spoke its language.

they cracked the buddha
& the mountain hollowed,

shadow collected on shadow
no one knew where to look.

ii.

who is they? oh me, oh mine.
this time. not another. this time

the blood of my blood, faith of my
faith. this time it is us in the mirror.

iii.

your name became mine & i forgot
my other loves. i looked down. before
me was you, before you was a life
that could be & i walked down that path,
at times i moved at the pace of a snail
at times i moved like a rapid, swallowing
current. could: what a foggy word. could:
land of the pure, land where we wouldn't
be hunted & skinned for the god we love.
could: us, a fairy tale i whispered to myself
every night. there was a sun in my legs
& i put it in your hands. there was a new
law & i obeyed. i obeyed.

iv.

the mountains, sky
rippled into curves

their snowy banks, rivers
running down their backs.

mountains that can't be moved
or owned, that break a man

& border, that tumble rock,
from the top, birds, eagle-winged,

flecked red & vast, circling.

v.

our prayers weaved with others.
the land who knew us,

the mountains that still call to me.

vi.

written down, things become
permanent. newspapers

announcing a new country, a new
name for god, all else falling away.

when you cheated on me
a knife punctured my border,

i couldn't speak the word
for days. when i texted

it to a friend, it became real,
the wind rewrote the dunes

the sand i carried in my chest.
spilled, my body now liquid,

my body opened by the naming.

[after, what remained?]

i.

me, alone. me, my own
new land

& body full of scabs.
not what had been,

emptied by a spell,
blank, so deep
in the dirt i was dirt.

ii.

in the hollows of the broken prophet
the shadows still carry secrets. keepers

of what was lost, keepers of time, softened
by talisman or a sweet word,

nectar on a poet's lips. the jinn move
& we quiet, the veil is thin at maghrib

right before the sun dies & leaves us
to the moon. they'll talk, the shadows, jinn,

if you let them in. madness & what lies before it,
wild as the tall grass & markhors' antlers.

[al-haq]

after the floods, people. after
the fires, people. not governments.

not borders. not the soldiers
or rifles. not the state

history or news or flag.
people, in masks,

cooking food, sorting rubble
& burned wood, driving to

each other, asking *are you
okay, baby?* when the sky

turned black, when the sun
went into the ocean,

when ash fell
instead of rain.

[i love them still]

my kin, my ripe bushel of apples,
orcharding, my wealth: ████
with the round face & always on
some kind of exercise routine. ████
name dripping silk, honey, a fat drop
of yogurt & blueberry. ████, who i haven't
seen in years but then looks up at me
from the photo in my baby album, ████,
who left me when i told my truth, who i knew
my words landed on like a knife, though
i did all i could to cut with flowers, bouquet
after bouquet. ████, who i left & missed
with each footstep, would wake in the night
confused, calling her name. the years make
long our distance, when i see her again
we're strangers, talking about the people
in our lives like they're characters in a tv show.
our worlds, fiction to each other, the raging
ocean between us, a murder of marine
life. cut me open & there they are: the ones
who left me, the ones i left, the roots
that ground me, the wind combing
my hair. & ████, who scared
me across the country for a decade, scattered
me like a seed. i still dream of the world

where i could've been his daughter. my ripe.
my beautiful apple. i still dream
of the world where he calls & i answer.

[beloved]

my father met you
at the grave & said no

my ancestors do not play
about me, their land

theirs, their laws their own
& etched in my body, full

of whispers & a song
only a few can sing.

my codes are changing,
mid-written, girled

but not fully. never-daughter
never-wife, a month short of son

& still my dead dad's name pops
up on the uber i call to flee

from you, flee from our shared home
& burrow my sleep into a hotel

pillow. rest foreigns my tongue.
in any language, the world

of dreams needs a legend,
cartographer & prayer wind

to lead the ship to shore.
even after death, my mom

meets my friend at her
grave & says no, the friend

bursting out of my life
like a firework, too loud

the sky a mess of light
& smoke on my fingers.

i used to hold on to everyone.
my body, a ghost-house

the key copied & passed between
hands. i thought i could love

them out of their mistakes.
i named their mistakes my own.

i gave my mistakes to them as gifts
& when they refused,

i covered their bodies with my name.
i promised my map, my whole,

the constellations in my sky
i kept a monster tamed

in my chest, a pit of faces,
demons in my sleep. they all

left anyways. the pit stayed.
all the leaving enough to make

anyone go mad. my list
whittled, small, loud as my pulse

you're protected, krista said.
my ancestors got loud

when it got quiet. am i mad
or am i just listening

for the first time?
in the grove of redwoods

my dad asked to be called
first & so i did, call. i called

& cried & begged for him
& oh, did he answer.

when you came, he roared.

[of course]

                there is god
but there are also people.

people flawed as people are
people who break things

on accident & on purpose.
in the land of mine, peepul

trees line the streets. king
of wood, king of branch

cleaning the air. the river's
stink. trash on the ground.

you, a person as all people are. you
who threw your arms wildly

& didn't look where they landed.
my body a person. my body a landing.

people threw trash on the land.
the land, a being. the land garbaged.

was it on purpose? was it
an accident? the mistakes

enough to break a camel.
the mistakes, mistaken.

you, a peepul. me, in the
land of mine. flawed. as

people. broken. breathing
street. cleaning air.

what we do to the earth we do
to each other. original mother.

the people trashed & there is only
land. garbage, a being, broken.

wood & king. my body,
a heart. my body. ache.

stinking, like the river.

[tracing]

i learn about her, my great-grandmother
without a name, bibi, kashmiri; sold

into marriage. *we don't know her ancestors,*
my uncle tells me. only her struggle

birthed in poverty & traded,
only to have her husband

die & all the coins she hid in jars
taken by her kin. pity: the story told

of her. poor, owned, dead husband
& too many kids. barely

even a story, just a collection of misery.
by the mountains, i hear her call to me.

i left you a map. but i'm hardheaded &
can't tell my right from my left. i pray

to each direction but get lost on the same
route home. & my husband is gone

too, not dead, but off with someone
else. *i need more help,* i ask.

i need more help, i hear in reply.

[you]

in the hammock in brazil, i showed
you tobacco as i had learned her. you,
a smoker, but not knowing her like this.
puffing without inhaling, the smoke
spiraling softly to the sky. around us,
nests of caterpillars cocooned
chrysalises of their own becoming.
like them, we were becoming.
you & i, becoming.

+

oh mother, of a land i cannot return to.
oh father, of a family i do not know.

oh country, oh border, oh law: renounce
the land of my father to have a shot at entering

the land of my mother. give up the unknown
for the chance at return. oh mother. oh father.

oh choice, oh end, oh begin, open, open, open.

+

+

in the wild of the jungle, i confessed
i was at a door, banging, that would not
open. *there's no way into kashmir*

i can see. months of meetings
with every organization
& being told no. my dream:

to be important enough to cross
a border. to be so important
i could go home. there was no

way in. in my shadow, in the dark side
of the mountain, i ignored a family
alive & waiting for a home where

no one would remember my name.
my father's call in the redwoods.
what about my kin   why

only your mother's   at atheel's wedding
she vowed *i used to think freedom*
was the choice to have it all. i realized

freedom is the ability to say, it is you, it is
this one choice, that i choose.

+

i prayed for love & saw a horse carrying
me to a cottage. we rode horses through
a jungle & river & i chose you. you, picking
the fattest book at the library to read. threading
the name of my mama's land into your flag.
hanging up a duvet as a painting. you; leather
biker's jacket, you; doing sit-ups while the dog
jumped on your chest. you; who i chose.
you; standing at the shrine to bad boys.

+

what i chose—my father, after years of pining
for my mother. you, after years of pining for the
ones who claimed to love me. writing the book
when i didn't know where it would lead. saying
i didn't know. a friend over the project. myself
over the friend. you over me. & finally, me over you.

+

you made homecoming
possible. you opened
the window when it was
stuck. you went through
& held out your hand. you
helped thread part of the needle.
we walked in the village

& no one would talk to me.
you said, *this is my wife. yes,*
this is my wife.

& i believed.

+

when you called me wife
everyone beamed & said
mashallah. the soft praise
to god, protecting us
golden-threaded & following
as we walked the streets,

i think everyone here loves love
you said, dimple in your cheek,
laugh rasping the field between us.

+

oh, your rasp.
your scratched
voice, my little

charmander.
in your throat,
running, the child

in you, fire-born
& wild.
voice smoked

dipped in
mezcal, like it
was made to burn.

+

in the best of the dreams
i wake & we are still ours.

you are not the past, not
something i'm trying to forget.

mundane, we pack for another
trip. *where are we going?* i ask

& you do not answer.

+

when you chose her, i was
in the house alone. the door
wouldn't open. i banged
& banged. i said no & still
you brought her in. the window

was stuck. the smoke rose. *wife.*
what a small word. thinning to air.

thinning to fucking air.

\+

after you left, my body
hollowed. my me left.

i was a body, without you
as i had been before, but

felt wrong. i forgot how to eat. i didn't
sleep. but i sat, kuripe in my palm.

stilling the war in my mind.
you, who i would have given

my voice just to keep
our little lie, our little life.

\+

in islam the angels are
terrifying, horned & black-winged,

scaled like dragons. power,
like love, will make you throw up.

+

when you came, the glass on the altar
broke. i pulled cards & claimed

expansion. when you came, i woke.
years of dusted living blew off my bones.

when you came, i prayed for softness.
let them be someone i can love for a long time.

+

for a while, the prayer held & then
it didn't. i shot the arrow

& missed. i had to root in the woods
& make sure i didn't kill something

else. in the spell of love, my sight
blurred. in the spell of love, i had

no aim.

+

if the angels are not concerned
with being pretty, then why

am i? the red on my lips
smearing the glass

on my teeth, on your cheek
in the photos, marking you.

mine, until you wash it off.
mine, until you leave.

+

the first time i met love, real love,
i got on my knees & apologized

for my life before. every mistake
i'd made illuminated by its light.

it came through the earth,
my ancestors lining up one

after another, a long curve
of those i'd forgotten & those

whose names i never knew.
the mountain's jagged light.

the mountains, saying, *you are ours.*
all the love i thought i'd met before

just guesswork, an approximation
a broken compass, a struggling poem.

no human could give me that, only
khuda, a field so bright i wondered

how i could never meet it before.
irresponsible, my tiny heart

breaks, how i mistook my small
flame for wildfire.

+

once, i knew you & then i did not.
simple. once you knew me

& then i was a stranger. once
you held the part of me that

i did not let others see & i held
yours. once, i kept your secrets.

i cradled you in the soft side
of my mountain, i took the sun

so you could sleep. i convinced
the stones. i gave them my honey.

i whispered *please.*

+

under the sun nothing is safe.
on top, the mountain witnesses

all & still stands. the heat loud, a sun
in the north & the south & the west & the east.

in sight, there is nowhere for darkness to hide.
even the soft turn of my wrist, loud

& written down, accounted for. even
you, back towards me, moving

on your own, singing a song
i do not know, a song i cannot hear.

+

when you left, the sky went out.
when you left, i was in my own

gorge, i had a mountain to climb.
when you left, i couldn't find

the candle. when you left, my friends
couldn't see my eyes. when you left

hours slipped & i lost where i was.
when you left, a valley of shadow

opened & called my name, a valley
of tears allah either did or did not see.

to open your heart, it needs
to break, my teacher said. oh.

oh. every thorn is breathing
in the wind. can't you see?

i'm wearing my skin inside out.
i'm breathing with my blood.

[i risked]

& you
contributed

to my library
of love. we planted

a tree that blossomed
in the springtime

before death clawed
through the park.

all love is a gamble.
i played with dice & fire.

in my garden
of forgiveness, i hold

a shovel in my palms.
your name

on my tongue. you
taste like prayer

& the earth is god.
i'm a little bitch

at the altar of beauty.
can you see what i

see? the rot at the root
but the flowers

are still in full bloom.
i'm on my knees.

allah, once again
i'm on my knees.

poem publication list;

the following poems have been published elsewhere, sometimes
with other titles.

[still life, interrupted by border]   in   *acacia*

[you]   in   *colorado review*

[from]   in   *ninth letter*

[armor]   in   *nour*

[my father was not the eldest]   in   *orion*

[museum]   in   *pocket stars*, edited by andrea
                                               lawlor (to be published by
                                               pantheon in spring 2027)

[i don't know what will kill us   in   poem-a-day
first: the race war or what we've
done to this earth]

[smell is the last memory to go] & in   poetry foundation
[i won't forget] &
[he was chaotic] &
[the women in my family]

[verily, i release] &   in   *prayers for the end of the*
[somewhere, somewhere,   *world and beginning of the*
someone]   *next*

[he made a movie.   in   *the adroit journal*
it was a flop.] &
[village boy]

[when we thought the world   in   *the american poetry review*
would end] &
[the ocean's tryna fuck]

[no one can take my anger] &   in   *the common*
[madness] &
[pagamento] &
[freedom song]

[they're in their lord of the flies   in   *the nation*
bag]

[& what a miracle]   in   *the shade journal*

[ya latif, ya latif, ya latif]   in   *wasafiri*

[museum] & [everyone grieves at the walk light] are ekphrasis poems based off Salman Toor paintings.

[when the army comes, the men disappear] came to me after reading "Half-Widows in Kashmir" by Mohammed Shahrukh in the Brown History Newsletter.

[pagamento] came after, & was heavily influenced by, a Pagamento Ceremony with the Mamos & Zagas of the Teyuna people in the Sierra Nevada de Santa Marta in Colombia. many of these lines are inspired by our collective prayers in that ceremony. i owe an incredible debt to the Mamos & Zagas, to the Teyuna people for their wisdom & to the mountains & land with which they are in relationship.

acknowledgments;

i am forever indebted to people & communities who have protected
their indigeneity from state violence & erasure, & who have shared
that protected knowledge as a way to help us all decolonize, & who
are the leaders of protecting this earth against climate change.

gratitude to my readers: sam sax, safia elhillo, hieu minh nguyen,
perry janes & kaveh akbar.

gratitude to the whole team at one world & nicole counts, my editor.
gratitude to my agent, pj mark.

thank you to zainab syed & fareed agha, who made reconnecting
with pakistan, & my family, possible.

with deep deep gratitude to all of my friends & family,

& particularly to hanif abdurraqib, angel nafis, shira erlichman, eve
ewing, jamila woods, randa jarrar, hollis wong-wear, chani nicholas,
sonya passi, terence nance, atheel elmalik, danez smith, chris gabo,
reva santo, josé olivarez, diamond sharp, esperanza spalding, fran
tirado, brontë velez, j wortham, sara elise, hala alyan, sarah kay,
qurissy lopez, dominique james, sherif ibrahim, nate marshall,
franny choi, vyvy trinh, pidgeon pagonis, kaveh akbar, safia elhillo,
hieu minh nguyen & sam sax for helping me when i needed it, when
i struggled to find the light.

about the author

FATIMAH ASGHAR, author of *If They Come for Us* and *When We Were Sisters,* is a poet, filmmaker, educator, and performer. They are the writer and co-creator of *Brown Girls,* an Emmy-nominated web series that highlights friendships between women of color. Along with Safia Elhillo, they are the editor of *Halal If You Hear Me,* an anthology that celebrates Muslim writers who are also women, queer, gender nonconforming, and/or trans. They were a co-producer of *Ms. Marvel* for Disney+ and wrote the episode "Time and Again."

Instagram, Threads, and X: @asgharthegrouch
fatimahasghar.com

about the type

This book was set in Fairfield, the first typeface from the hand of
the distinguished American artist and engraver Rudolph Ruzicka
(1883–1978). Ruzicka was born in Bohemia (in the present-day
Czech Republic) and came to America in 1894. He set up his own
shop, devoted to wood engraving and printing, in New York in 1910
after a varied career working as a wood engraver, in photoengraving
and banknote printing plants, and as an art director and freelance
artist. He designed and illustrated many books, and was the creator
of a considerable list of individual prints—wood engravings, line
engravings on copper, and aquatints.